# COBBLESTONE® · THE CIVIL WAR

# Robert E. Lee
## Duty and Honor

**Cobblestone Publishing**
**A Division of Carus Publishing**
**Peterborough, NH**
**www.cobblestonepub.com**

**Staff**

Editorial Director: Lou Waryncia

Editor: Sarah Elder Hale

Book Design: David Nelson, www.dnelsondesign.com

Proofreaders: Meg Chorlian, Eileen Terrill

**Text Credits**

The content of this volume is derived from articles that first appeared in *COBBLESTONE* magazine. Contributors: Brenda Brotomer, Virginia Calkins, Sarah Elder Hale, Harold Holzer, Joan Hunt, Brandon Marie Miller, Mark Travis, Shari Lyn Zuber

**Picture Credits**

Photos.com: 3, 6, 15, 38–39; Library of Congress: 4, 9, 10, 11, 12 (bottom), 13 (center), 18, 19, 20, 21, 23 (top), 25, 26 (bottom), 27, 28, 30–31, 32, 34, 35, 36, 37, 40, 42 (bottom), 43; Lee Chapel, Washington and Lee University: 5, 8, 12 (top); Courtesy of the Robert E. Lee Memorial Association, Stratford Hall Plantation: 7; Collections of the Virginia Historical Society, Richmond, Va.: 13 (top), 13 (bottom); National Archives: 14; Fred Carlson: 16–17, 44–45; Clipart.com: 22, 23 (bottom), 24, 26 (top), 33, 41, 42 (top). Images for "Civil War Time Line," pages 44–45, courtesy of Photos.com, Clipart.com, and Library of Congress.

**Cover**

Charles Hoffbauer, *The Four Seasons of the Confederacy*, Summer Mural

Collections of Virginia Historical Society/Center for Virginia History

**Copyright © 2005 Carus Publishing Company**

**Library of Congress Cataloging-in-Publication Data**

Robert E. Lee : duty and honor / [project editor, Lou Waryncia ; editor, Sarah Elder Hale].

    p. cm. — (Cobblestone the Civil War)

    Includes index.

    ISBN 0-8126-7905-9 (hardcover)

Lee, Robert E. (Robert Edward), 1807–1870—Juvenile literature. 2. Generals Confederate States of America—Biography—Juvenile literature. 3. Confederate States of America. Army—Biography—Juvenile literature. 4. United States—History—Civil War, 1861–1865—Juvenile literature.

I. Waryncia, Lou. II. Hale, Sarah Elder. III. Title. IV. Series.

    E467.1.L4R624 2005

    973.7'3'092—dc22                                 2005015824

**Printed in China**

**Cobblestone Publishing**

30 Grove Street, Suite C

Peterborough, NH 03458

www.cobblestonepub.com

# Table of Contents

The Lee ancestral home, Stratford Hall Plantation, near Fredericksburg in eastern Virginia, was built in the 1730s. Robert E. Lee was born there on January 19, 1807.

# Fallen Family

**O**n June 18, 1793, at her family's red-brick plantation house overlooking the James River, Ann Hill Carter married Revolutionary War hero Henry "Light-Horse Harry" Lee. Although the Lees were one of Virginia's first families, Harry's money problems were well known, and the Carters did not approve of 20-year-old Ann's decision to marry him. Their concern was warranted.

## In Debt

Less than 10 years into their marriage, despite a sparkling political and military career, Harry was tens of thousands of dollars in debt because of bad investments. He was forced to sell most of the family lands under his control. Ann's father was so concerned about Harry's behavior that he rewrote his will so that Ann's and her children's inheritances would be safe from the "possession or molestation from her husband, General Lee."

By 1806, despite the family's dire financial circumstances, Ann and Harry had four children: Algernon Sydney (who died in childhood), Charles Carter, Ann Kinloch, and Sydney Smith. Their fifth child was born on January 19, 1807, shortly after the death of Ann's beloved father. The boy was named Robert Edward after two of Ann's brothers. A sixth child, Mildred, was born in 1811.

## Key Players

# Henry "Light-Horse Harry" Lee
### 1756–1818

**H**enry Lee III, a respected cavalry hero during the American Revolution, was a daring soldier and expert horseman. His friends called him "Light-Horse Harry" Lee, a nickname that stayed with him all his life. After the Revolution, Lee served in Congress and later as governor of Virginia, and always maintained a strong friendship with George Washington.

He had been married only eight years when his first wife, Matilda, died, leaving him with three young children. To add to his grief, his eldest child died a short time later. In 1793, three years after Matilda's death, Henry married Ann Hill Carter.

Throughout his marriage, Henry was plagued with financial problems that became a constant source of stress and instability. His heavy debts, unpopular political views, and ill health isolated him from his family and friends for the remainder of his life.

When Robert was two, his father was arrested and sent to prison for not paying his debts. Harry spent his time in prison writing his memoirs of the Revolutionary War. Ann's family encouraged her to leave him, but she refused. "Mr. Lee," she wrote, "constantly assures me his intention is to live with his family after his release from his present situation."

## A Fresh Start

Shortly after Harry's release from prison in 1810, the Lees moved to the Potomac River city of Alexandria, just outside the new capital of Washington, D.C. There, the children could go to school, and Ann could be closer to Lee and Carter relatives.

With Ann's income from her father and the generosity of relatives, Ann and Harry began a new life in Alexandria. But Harry hated living so close to people who looked at him with pity or disdain. He blamed others for his lack of success and in July 1812 traveled to Baltimore to help a journalist friend who opposed America's new war with Britain. An angry pro-war mob attacked the two men, and Harry barely escaped with his life. In May 1813, still suffering from health problems stemming from his wounds, he went into exile in the Caribbean. Occasionally, he sent his family letters and gifts. In one letter, he asked Carter to "hug my dear Robert for me and kiss little Mildred," although he barely knew his two youngest children.

A Lee relative arranged for Ann and the children to move into a large home at 607 Oronoco Street. By 1816, Ann was feeling the pinch of an economic depression. Her brother helped by sending Carter to Harvard. Ann wrote Carter urging him to economize as his mother, brothers, and sisters did each evening when they decided how to spend their few cents for the next day's food.

As for Harry, the family never saw him again; he tried to return to Virginia in 1818, but died making the trip.

Through all the trials of her marriage and motherhood, Ann Lee instilled in her children a firm sense of honor and discipline. With the death of her husband, her health continued to decline, and she eventually required regular care. Thirteen-year-old Robert, the last son at home, provided much of the nursing. He was by her bedside when she died in 1829, shortly after his graduation from West Point military academy.

Harry Lee was plagued by debt, and Ann had to rely on the generosity of family and friends to keep her family out of poverty.

# Young Robert

**L**ittle is known about Robert E. Lee's childhood. His half-brother, Henry Lee IV (from Harry's first marriage), recalled Robert greeting him looking "sheepish and shamefaced," trying to hide a lost tooth with a bone replacement that would not stay in place. He enjoyed the time he could spend with his many cousins on both sides of his family, Lee and Carter. He was accomplished at skating, and loved swimming in the Potomac River; he was an excellent dancer, and shared an affinity for horses that he must have inherited from his father.

Even as a child, Robert worked hard at being good. He excelled in school, studying Latin, Greek, and math. In early 1824, 17-year-old Robert applied to the U.S. Military Academy at West Point. The academy provided a free education and a career. Ann was now suffering from tuberculosis and spending time at a relative's house in the country. She wrote her son Smith, who was away in the navy, "Alas, alas, I wish I had my little boys Smith and Robert living with me again." She lived long enough to know that Robert graduated second in his class at West Point.

As an adult, Robert wrote, "A child learns all that it has of good from its mother." He fretted over his own children's upbringing and preached duty, self-denial, and discipline. From a troubled childhood, he emerged to rescue the tarnished Lee name, becoming the most famous son of a famous American family.

**Fast Fact**

Robert was

**11**

when his father died. He visited his father's grave in Dungeness, Georgia, for the first time in 1862, when he was

**55.**

Robert could draw well and gave this drawing of a turtle to a young woman in Savannah, Georgia.

# Soldier of Honor

The summer sun shone brightly as 18-year-old Robert Edward Lee disembarked from the steamship that had brought him up New York State's Hudson River to the U.S. Military Academy at West Point. The academy's beautiful but Spartan grounds were but a foreshadowing of the harsh lifestyle that awaited the young Virginian. Yet his difficult youth had prepared him well for what lay ahead.

This portrait of Robert E. Lee in dress uniform was painted about 1831, while Lee was a lieutenant in the Army Corps of Engineers.

## Model Student and Officer

Of the 87 young men who began their education with Lee in 1825, only he and 45 others would graduate in 1829. Lee graduated second in his class, and he was the first student to graduate from West Point without a single demerit (a mark against a cadet because of a rule violation).

Because of his standing, Lee was appointed to the elite U.S. Army Corps of Engineers. The War of 1812 had shown that the United States needed a strong Atlantic coastal defense; so, the government authorized a plan to build 200 forts along the eastern seaboard (only 30, however, were completed before the outbreak of the Civil War). Lee's first assignment as a new lieutenant was to aid in the construction of Fort Pulaski on Cockspur Island, near Savannah, Georgia. The project's commander, Samuel Babcock, was in poor health and passed most of his responsibilities to the 22-year-old officer. Lee ably supervised the project and learned how to exercise authority.

Over the next 16 years, Lee was reassigned to oversee upgrades of several coastal fortifications, from Fort Monroe at the entrance to Chesapeake Bay to Fort Hamilton in Brooklyn, New York.

In 1835, Lee was headed to the Midwest to survey the Ohio–Michigan border, and during the summer of 1836, he was given the monumental task of rerouting the Mississippi River to prevent the destruction of the city of St. Louis. Lee, with fellow Army engineer Montgomery Meigs, devised a series of dikes that deflected the river's currents and stopped the formation of sandbars, which would have isolated the city from river traffic. For his success, he was promoted to captain.

## The U.S.–Mexican War

In 1845, the independent Republic of Texas was annexed by the United States, provoking a border dispute with Mexico. Lee reported to San Antonio, Texas, in September 1846, and began serving under General John E. Wool. For the next three months, Lee led engineers in building bridges, improving roads, and removing the obstacles to Mexico.

Wool's inability to locate Mexican general Santa Anna's forces led to Lee's acting as scout. With just a young Mexican as a guide, Lee pinpointed the

## U.S. Military Academy at West Point

**S**ince its founding in 1802, West Point military academy has trained young men (and, since 1975, women) to be U.S. Army officers of the highest caliber. Applicants to West Point must be 17 to 22 years of age, be good students, and pass physical qualifications. Also, applicants must be nominated by the president, vice president, or a member of Congress. Once an applicant is chosen, he or she attends West Point with a full scholarship. The four-year program is rigorous, emphasizing discipline and excellence. At graduation, cadets become fully commissioned officers of the U.S. Army.

United States military history is full of stories of West Point graduates. Many of the generals who served in the Civil War, Union and Confederate, graduated from West Point. Both Robert E. Lee and his Union rival Ulysses S. Grant were proud alumni of West Point and products of the same military training. When Lee chose to support the Southern states that seceded from the Union and join the army of the Confederate States of America, he sadly resigned his commission in the U.S. Army.

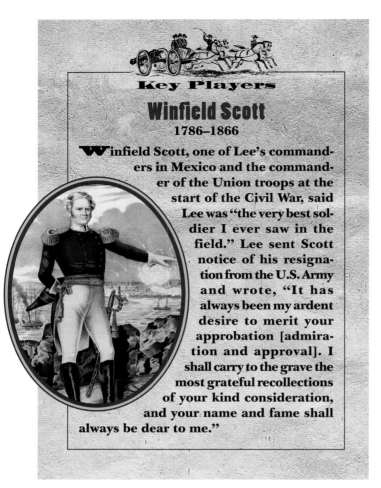

enemy and then rode 40 miles back to camp. With only a three-hour rest, he led the U.S. troops to the enemy campsite, which ensured General Zachary Taylor's success at Buena Vista.

At the special request of General Winfield Scott, Lee joined his command and supervised the construction of the gun batteries that assisted in the capture of Veracruz, Mexico. Further distinguishing himself at Cerro Gordo, Lee made it possible for American troops and equipment to scale the mountain fortress village and surprise Santa Anna by attacking from the rear.

He also found a route through a supposedly impassable lava bed, clearing the way to Mexico City. For his services at the Battle of Chapultepec (the fortified steep hill protecting the Mexican capital), Lee was promoted to brevet colonel.

## Crisscrossing the Country

With the war's end, Lee once again returned to fort construction duty, until his appointment as superintendent of West Point in 1852. There, Lee tightened the school's budget, modernized the curriculum, and improved cadet uniforms and living quarters. Although he was a strong leader, he did his best to err on the side of the student and always regretted having to give a demerit or dismiss a cadet.

The development of new regiments to police the expanding western frontier resulted in Lee's reassignment to Texas in 1855 as a lieutenant colonel in the 2nd Cavalry. However, the death of his wife's father in 1857 required that Lee take a two-year leave of

absence to settle estate problems at Arlington, the family home
in Virginia.

In October 1859, Lee commanded a force of U.S. Marines to the
site of the U.S. military garrison at Harpers Ferry, Virginia, where
he suppressed an uprising led by abolitionist John Brown, who with
his followers had seized the armory for weapons to incite a slave
revolt. Lee then returned to duty in San Antonio to command the
headquarters of the Department of Texas.

In February 1861, General Scott ordered him back to Washington.
Since Abraham Lincoln's election, Southern states had been
seceding from the Union. Lee was offered command of the Union
forces. For the first time in his career, he was forced to decide where
his greater loyalty lay — with the country he had served for 32 years
or with his ancestral state. Lee's father, Light-Horse Harry Lee,
had once said, "Virginia is my country; her I will obey, however
lamentable the fate to which it may subject me." So was the choice
made by the son.

**At Veracruz, Lee
supervised the gun
batteries that were
used for the bombard-
ment of the city. Lee's
brother Sydney Smith
Lee was one of the
naval officers who
helped coordinate
transferring cannon
from the ships to
the shore.**

# A Lee Family Album

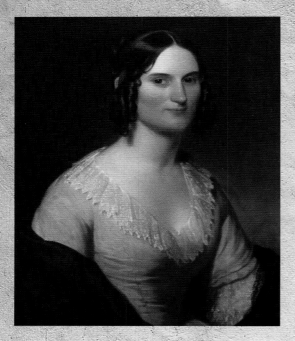

## Marriage and Children

**A**round 1830, young Robert E. Lee, newly graduated from West Point military academy, began courting Mary Anna Randolph Custis. The daughter of Martha Washington's grandson, Mary was an aristocratic and temperamental girl. Over her father's initial objections, she and Lee were married in June 1831. The Lees had seven children, three boys and four girls: George Washington Custis, Mary Custis, William Henry Fitzhugh, Anne (Annie) Carter, Eleanor Agnes, Robert, Jr., and Mildred (Milly) Childe.

## A Museum of a Home

**A**rlington, the Lees' home in northern Virginia, was a grand residence. With its front entrance framed by eight thick pillars, it looked more like a monument than a home. In fact, it was a monument. Lee's wife, Mary Custis, was a descendant of Martha Washington, and Arlington had been built as a museum honoring her husband, George. It was filled with the Washingtons' belongings.

## Loving Father

**I**n 1853, while he was serving as superintendent of West Point, Lee wrote Annie, "Oh, what pleasure I lose in being separated from my children! Nothing can compensate me for that." Lee made up endearing nicknames for his children, calling Custis "Boo," William "Rooney," Agnes "Wiggie," and Mildred "Precious Life" (shown here with her mother). Yet he always demanded, and received, proper obedience. When Rooney, the most unruly of the three sons, accidentally cut off several fingertips, Lee blamed himself and used the incident to stress the value of obedience to his other children. His youngest son, Robert, Jr., once wrote, "I always knew that it was impossible to disobey my father."

## War and Worry

**A**ll three of Lee's sons served in the Confederate army. His eldest child, Custis (shown here with his father), rose to a general's rank during the Civil War and was the only son to become a career soldier.

During the Civil War, Lee worried more for his family than for himself. His wife, Mary, was in poor health and had to keep to her bed for long periods of time. In 1862, tragedy struck when 23-year-old Annie died of typhoid fever. Upon hearing the news, Lee wrote that there was "nothing to lighten the full weight of my grief." Lee's other difficulties included the death of a grandson and the wounding and capture of Rooney during the war.

## Dutiful Daughters

**A**gnes, or "Wiggie," enjoyed reading, music, and working in her garden. She kept a journal throughout her childhood years that was later published, titled *Growing Up in the 1850s*.

Whereas Lee encouraged his sons to marry, he was unwilling to share his daughters' affection with anyone. Despite their complaints, they honored their father's desire that they stay home and care for their parents, and they never married.

# John Brown Stirs Things Up

In 1859, two factors came together with explosive results: a man passionately opposed to slavery, and a small town guarding a huge supply of weapons and ammunition. John Brown's decision to seize federal weapons at Harpers Ferry, Virginia (in present-day West Virginia), set a match to the powderkeg issue that was dividing the Northern and Southern states: slavery.

## Man With a Mission

John Brown was a militant abolitionist who proposed a radical strategy to run slaves off their Virginia plantations. His plan involved stationing bands of armed men (antislavery whites and runaway slaves) at intervals in the Allegheny Mountains from

Virginia to Pennsylvania. Fugitive slaves could either join the slave army or escape north by the Underground Railroad.

Abolitionist Frederick Douglass, an African American, described Brown, "Though a white gentleman, [he] is in sympathy a black man, and as deeply interested in our cause, as though his own soul had been pierced with the iron of slavery."

In 1855, Brown led the fight against proslavery Missourians and Southerners fighting to bring Kansas into the Union as a slave state. A poor man himself, he traveled back and forth across the eastern half of the country soliciting money and weapons. Douglass gathered audiences to hear Brown's appeals for funds for Kansas, but Douglass noted that Brown "never lost sight of what he called his greater work — the liberation of all the slaves in the United States."

## 'A Perfect Steel Trap'

By 1858, Brown's plan expanded to include seizing the U.S. weapons arsenal at Harpers Ferry, which amounted to a direct attack on the federal government. Douglass advised against it, stating, "You're walking into a perfect steel trap, and you will never get out alive."

Despite Douglass's advice and delays in executing his raid, Brown and 21 of his followers entered the town at dawn on October 16, 1859. They cut telegraph wires and broke into the arsenal and the local riflemaker's shop. They seized white hostages, hoping to embolden the local slaves to join their fight. None did, and the town militia soon had Brown and his men cornered.

An alert was sent to Washington by way of a passing freight train, and President James Buchanan quickly dispatched two companies of soldiers under the command of Colonel Robert E. Lee. Between the local force and Lee's troops, John Brown's insurrection was quickly silenced. Brown lost 10 men in the skirmish, and he was arrested on a charge of treason. His trial was swift and the sentence severe: execution. Brown was hanged on December 2.

News of John Brown's daring plot intensified the slavery debate. The Civil War did not officially begin until April 1861, but for Robert E. Lee the first shots were fired at Harpers Ferry.

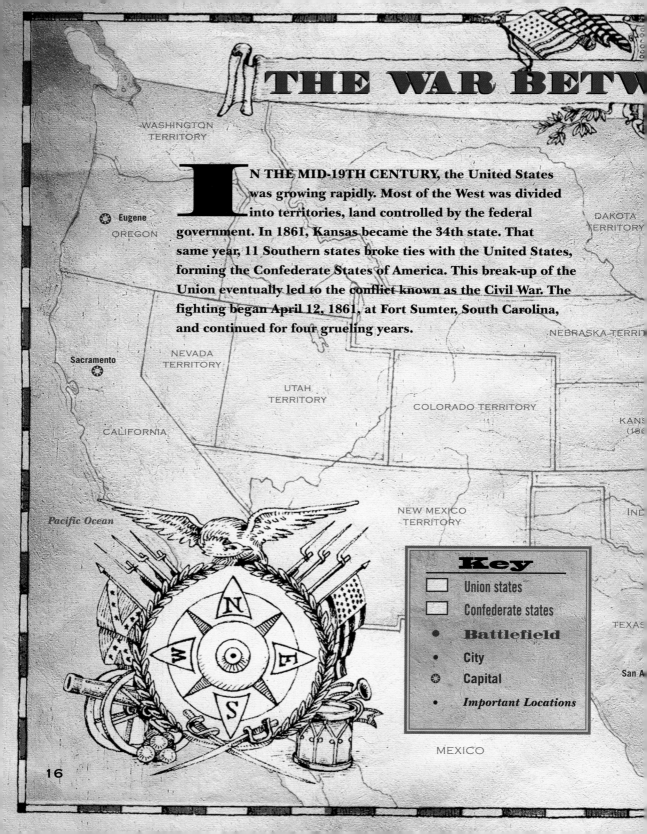

WASHINGTON
TERRITORY

⊛ Eugene
OREGON

DAKOTA
TERRITORY

**I**N THE MID-19TH CENTURY, the United States
was growing rapidly. Most of the West was divided
into territories, land controlled by the federal
government. In 1861, Kansas became the 34th state. That
same year, 11 Southern states broke ties with the United States,
forming the Confederate States of America. This break-up of the
Union eventually led to the conflict known as the Civil War. The
fighting began April 12, 1861, at Fort Sumter, South Carolina,
and continued for four grueling years.

NEBRASKA TERRIT

Sacramento
⊛

NEVADA
TERRITORY

UTAH
TERRITORY

COLORADO TERRITORY

KANS
(186

CALIFORNIA

Pacific Ocean

NEW MEXICO
TERRITORY

IND

### Key

☐ Union states

☐ Confederate states

● **Battlefield**

• City

⊛ Capital

• *Important Locations*

TEXAS

San A

MEXICO

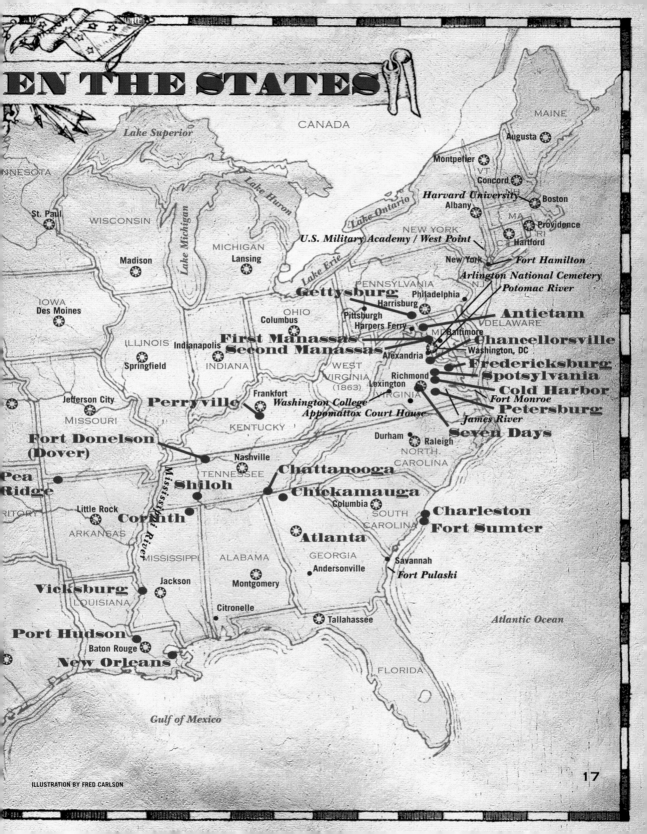

# EN THE STATES

ILLUSTRATION BY FRED CARLSON

17

Robert E. Lee wrote to his sister in 1861, "Save in defense of my native state,…I hope I may never be called on to draw my sword." When Virginia joined the Confederacy, Lee felt bound by loyalty to fight for the South.

# The Civil War Years

## 1861: Called to Command

**A**s hard as it is to imagine, Robert E. Lee spent the first year of the Civil War in obscurity. He did nothing heroic, nothing dramatic. He was merely in charge of the defense of western Virginia, and he even proved unable to prevent Union forces from seizing that territory.

Many in the Confederacy concluded that Lee had grown too old for important command. His critics called him "Evacuating Lee" and "Granny Lee." Few Southerners in 1861 would have guessed that he would soon emerge as the greatest Confederate military hero of the war.

Ironically, Northerners seemed to appreciate Lee before Southerners did. President Abraham Lincoln offered him command of all Union forces in early 1861, but Lee declined. He said that he would never raise his sword against his native state, and by then Virginia had seceded to join the Confederacy. Lee

### Fort Sumter

**F**ort Sumter, a Union stronghold guarding the port of Charleston, South Carolina, was the first target of the Confederate forces. The fort's commanding officer, Major Robert Anderson, refused to turn over control of the fort to the newly formed Confederate States of America, and on April 12, 1861, Confederate general Pierre G.T. Beauregard led a full-scale attack. Unable to hold off the Confederates, Anderson was forced to surrender the following afternoon. The bombardment of Fort Sumter is generally accepted as the opening engagement of the Civil War.

For the next four years, Fort Sumter remained in Confederate hands despite repeated attempts by Union forces to regain control. All told, the fort absorbed some 46,000 hits by heavy artillery. When the South surrendered in 1865, ending the Civil War, Fort Sumter had been reduced to rubble and ruin. The federal government rebuilt the fort, and today it is a national monument.

returned home, believing he would fight no more.

## 1862: Victories in Virginia

Confederate president Jefferson Davis had faith in Lee when many others did not. Despite Lee's early failures in western Virginia, Davis made him his personal military advisor. Then, in the spring of 1862, Confederate general Joseph E. Johnston was gravely wounded in action, and Lee was named to take his place as commander of Confederate forces throughout the state.

It was a moment of crisis. Union troops seemed poised to take the Confederate capital of Richmond and win the war.

Now in command of the Army of Northern Virginia, Lee reorganized his force and summoned the legendary general Thomas J. "Stonewall" Jackson to join him. In the Seven Days Campaign that followed (June 25 to July 1), Lee turned back the much larger Union invasion force and sent it into retreat toward Washington, D.C.

That August, Lee again met Federal forces in the Second Battle of Manassas, Virginia (August 28–30), site of the war's first Confederate victory the year before. This time, with Lee in command, the Confederate triumph was even greater.

Confident that he could now invade the North and force Lincoln to end the fighting and recognize the Confederacy, Lee marched into Maryland. There he met Union forces at the fierce Battle of Antietam (September 17). It was the bloodiest day of the war. Nearly 23,000 soldiers were killed or wounded in the fighting.

**At Fredericksburg, Union troops used pontoon boats to bridge the Rappahannock River, while Lee's army fired upon them from the hills above town.**

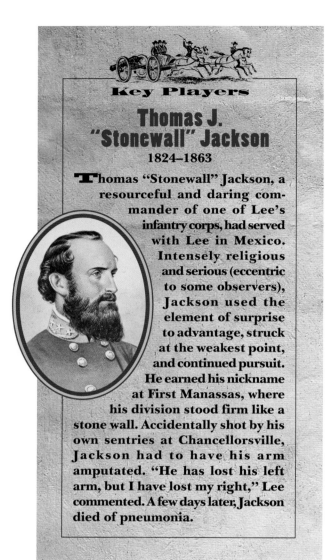

## Thomas J. "Stonewall" Jackson
### 1824–1863

Thomas "Stonewall" Jackson, a resourceful and daring commander of one of Lee's infantry corps, had served with Lee in Mexico. Intensely religious and serious (eccentric to some observers), Jackson used the element of surprise to advantage, struck at the weakest point, and continued pursuit. He earned his nickname at First Manassas, where his division stood firm like a stone wall. Accidentally shot by his own sentries at Chancellorsville, Jackson had to have his arm amputated. "He has lost his left arm, but I have lost my right," Lee commented. A few days later, Jackson died of pneumonia.

Although Lee commanded brilliantly, he was unable to defeat the enemy and was forced to retreat back into Virginia. Lee's defeat encouraged Lincoln to issue the Emancipation Proclamation a few days after the battle.

Three months later, Union forces marched on the Confederacy. On December 13, the two armies met at the Battle of Fredericksburg, where Lee dealt the North a crushing defeat. Cleverly positioned on the heights overlooking town, the Confederates were able to pick off Union troops as they crossed the Rappahannock River and attempted to scale the hills.

## 1863: Chancellorsville and Gettysburg

Robert E. Lee's masterpiece was the Battle of Chancellorsville in May 1863. There, a brilliant strategy produced a great victory for the South and a humiliating defeat for the North. But it was Lee who suffered the greatest loss of the day. His chief lieutenant general, Thomas "Stonewall" Jackson, was shot by his own men, who mistook him for a Union soldier, and died a few days later.

Rather than wait for the enemy to take advantage of this tragedy, Lee went on the offensive. He launched his second, and last, invasion of the North, reaching what became known as the "High Tide" of the Confederacy in July 1863 at the biggest and most famous encounter of the war, the Battle of Gettysburg in Pennsylvania. On the second day of furious fighting outside the sleepy village, Confederate forces failed to win the decisive high ground from the Union. Lee might have retreated that very afternoon, but he decided to gamble by ordering a massive attack the following day.

It was the most controversial decision of Lee's career. Pickett's Charge, as the assault became known, ended in a huge death toll and defeat, and Lee marched his beaten army south, never again to regain the glory of early 1863. The fact that he was able to save his army and bring it back to the South, however, was itself a triumph for Lee. Had Union troops pursued him, he would have been trapped by the floodwaters of the Potomac River. Forced to fight yet again, Lee might have been crushed, ending the war. But Union forces stayed put in Gettysburg, and Lee was able to escape.

Ulysses S. Grant became commander of all Union forces in March 1864.

## 1864: Lee Faces Grant

By this time, although Lee had become a beloved hero in the South, he had been slowed by advancing age and crippling heart

### Key Players
# Richard Stoddert Ewell
### 1817–1872

**R**ichard S. Ewell was known affectionately as "Old Bald Head" by his soldiers. At the Battle of Groveton (August 29, 1862), Ewell lost a leg and had to be strapped to his horse. In 1863, after Stonewall Jackson's death, Lee gave Ewell Jackson's 2nd Corps. Some blamed Ewell for the Confederate defeat at Gettysburg. He was captured at Sailor's (Sayler's) Creek in 1865.

## Key Players

# John Bell Hood
### 1831–1879

John B. Hood's early success as an Indian fighter in Texas was due to his aggressiveness, drive, and bravery. He always went into the thickest fire with his men. Among his most important contributions was his command of the Confederate army in the West during the battles of Atlanta (July 2, 1864), Franklin, Tennessee (November 30, 1864), and Nashville (December 15–16, 1864).

## Key Players

# James Longstreet
### 1821–1904

Steady, stubborn, and dependable, James Longstreet commanded one of Lee's infantry corps. Although he was accused of using excessive caution, especially at Gettysburg, his defensive brilliance at Fredericksburg and Antietam was unquestioned. Longstreet was a father figure to his soldiers, and Lee called him "my old war horse." To his soldiers, he was "Old Pete."

disease. Still, there was never any thought of replacing or even resting him. Somehow, he went on to face a Union army twice the size of his own when Ulysses S. Grant marched against Richmond in 1864. At the battles of the Wilderness, Spotsylvania, and Cold Harbor, Lee held Grant at bay, while 50,000 Union soldiers fell in action. But with supplies dwindling, his soldiers beginning to desert, and Northern replacements vastly outpacing his own troops, Lee knew he would be unable to survive.

Now the commander of all Confederate armies, he convinced his government to allow him to recruit slaves to fight for the South. Although this plan was never put into action, it would have been a cruel blow to African Americans, asking them to fight to save the system that held them in bondage. Although Lee did believe that slaves who served in the Confederate army should be freed, this proposal was not his finest moment.

## 1865: Surrender

In the spring of 1865, Lee was finally forced to surrender Richmond to the Union. He was no longer able to protect the capital. As Jefferson Davis and his government fled farther south, Lee made one final attempt to link up with Confederate forces in North Carolina. But Grant's troops surrounded and trapped Lee's men. The general had no other choice but to surrender his army, which now numbered only 28,000 exhausted, hungry, badly equipped men. Lee himself, though only 58 years old, had aged beyond his years. In just four years, he had changed from a robust middle-aged

Lee's army encountered Union generals Grant and Meade at the Wilderness in northern Virginia. The battle was a draw, but Lee was unable to stop Grant's advance on Richmond.

## James Ewell Brown 'J.E.B.' Stuart
### 1833—1864

"**J**.E.B." Stuart commanded the Confederate cavalry. Lee called him "the eyes and ears of my army," as his infallible intelligence-gathering activities became indispensable. He wore a satin-lined cape, feathered hat, and jingling spurs, which made him a favorite with the ladies. Dashing, with great physical strength and endurance, he was greatly missed after a clash with Union general Philip Sheridan's cavalry resulted in his death.

**Lee observes the Battle of Fredericksburg from the hills above town.**

man to an elderly-looking veteran with a thick white beard.

Although many historians believe that Lee erred twice by marching north on invasions doomed to failure, no one has ever questioned Lee's genius at command and his extraordinary ability to devise masterful battle strategies and inspire his men. He outguessed his opponents; knew precisely when to attack, wait, and counterattack; and chose brilliant and devoted field generals. Most remarkable of all, Lee won almost all his battles against much larger opposing armies, earning him a reputation as one of the greatest military leaders America has ever produced.

# Traveller

Of all his horses, Traveller was Lee's favorite. By the end of the war, Traveller was as well known as Lee himself.

**D**uring the fall of 1861, in the mountains of western Virginia, Robert E. Lee purchased a five-year-old gray horse, first named Jeff Davis and later Greenbrier. Renamed Traveller, this gallant animal unfailingly served Lee through the terrible years of the Civil War.

## The General's Favorite

Lee had four other horses in his entourage (Richmond, Ajax, Brown Roan, and Lucy Long), but the "Confederate Gray" soon became the

27

Lee (right) and General "Stonewall" Jackson (left) plan a battle astride their warhorses, Traveller and Little Sorrel.

general's favorite. Traveller stood 16 hands high (64 inches at the point of his shoulder). He was dark iron gray and had a black mane and tail. Even under the poorest conditions, when snow and mud were knee-deep and the only food was corncobs, this noble horse seemed untiring and always responsive to his master's commands.

Lee once wrote lovingly about how a painting of Traveller should look: "Such a picture would inspire a poet, whose genius could then depict his worth or describe his endurance of toil, hunger, thirst, heat and cold, and the dangers and sufferings through which he has passed."

## Admired by All

Eventually, the calm gray warhorse became as well known and recognizable to the Army of Northern Virginia as the general himself. Traveller accompanied Lee from Virginia to Georgia and north to Pennsylvania. In one letter home, he wrote that at Richmond, the "Gray" had carried him through seven days of battle, and in the campaign of 1864, the saddle was seldom off his back.

It was Traveller whom Lee rode to Appomattox Court House on

April 9, 1865. After accepting the surrender conditions of General Grant, Lee rode Traveller back to his troops. As their valiant commander passed by, many of the soldiers lovingly patted the flanks of the gray horse they knew so well.

## After the War

When Lee accepted the presidency of Washington College in Lexington, Virginia, Traveller continued to serve him. Before his family arrived in Lexington, he wrote, "Traveller is my only companion, I may also say my pleasure." Lee often took long rides, sometimes accompanied by his daughter on Lucy Long, who also had survived the war.

Lee would sometimes allow Traveller to graze on the lush green grass of his front lawn, believing that the horse deserved some pampering after the ordeal of the war. Lee's horse had become so famous that he was sent sets of saddles and bridles from England, Baltimore, and Richmond, though his favorite was thought to be an American saddle from St. Louis. During a holiday trip, Lee wrote to his clerk, "How is Traveller? Tell him I miss him dreadfully, and have repented of our separation but once — and this the whole time since we parted."

Traveller performed his final act of service for his master on October 15, 1870. The celebrated warhorse, with empty saddle and bridle draped in black crepe, was led by two Confederate veterans, following Lee's hearse to the college chapel.

Traveller survived his master by only two years. He contracted tetanus (lockjaw) from a nail that had penetrated his hoof and could not be saved. For years, Traveller's skeleton was displayed in the museum at Washington and Lee University. Now the warhorse is interred at the university near the tomb of the master he served so well.

## Lee's Chicken

**T**here's nothing like a fresh egg for breakfast — at least that's what General Robert E. Lee thought. During the Civil War, Lee traveled with a pet hen that laid an egg under the general's cot each morning.

### Fast Fact

Traveller was only

**11**

years old when he died, about half the average life span of a horse.

Ulysses S. Grant agreed to meet Robert E. Lee at Appomattox Court House, Virginia, to discuss the surrender of Lee's Army of Northern Virginia. The meeting took place at the home of Wilmer McLean.

# Dignity in Defeat

**R**obert E. Lee had become famous for the way he waged war. But he became even more famous — and more beloved — for the way he waged peace. Even though he was "vanquished," wrote his military aide, he seemed somehow "a victor."

## The War Is Lost

By 1865, the Civil War had been raging for four years. Poorly
clothed, inadequately armed, and ill fed, Confederate soldiers
began deserting in great numbers. Those who remained from
Lee's once-fearsome Army of Northern Virginia were soon
surrounded by superior Union forces under General Ulysses S.
Grant. In early April, Lee reluctantly came to the conclusion that
he must surrender to Grant before more lives were sacrificed to a
cause now hopelessly lost.

## The McLean House

**I**n 1861, Wilmer and Virginia McLean owned a home at Manassas, Virginia, the site of the first battle of the war (after the attack on Fort Sumter). When the guns were finally quiet, they decided to move away so that they would never be in the midst of war again. It's a good thing they did, because a second battle was fought on the same site in 1862. However, escaping the war was not so easy for the McLeans. In one of history's great ironies, the McLeans' new home in Appomattox Court House, Virginia, was the location of Lee's surrender to Union general Ulysses S. Grant. The war that began in the McLeans' front yard ended in their parlor.

At first, Lee proposed that Grant meet him to discuss peace terms, but the Union commander refused. There could be no discussion, only surrender. Lee might simply have sent word that he was giving up and returned home to his family. But he probably remembered that the famous British general Lord Cornwallis had been much criticized for refusing to attend the ceremony of his surrender to George Washington during the Revolutionary War.

Lee decided he would personally surrender his army, just as Grant desired.

## Day of Surrender

On April 9, Lee donned a glorious new full-dress uniform, placed a gleaming sword at his side, and rode slowly to the place that had been chosen for the ceremony: the home of a man named Wilmer McLean in the town of Appomattox Court House, Virginia. The town was about 120 miles from the place where the first battle of the war had been fought four years earlier.

Lee's appearance shocked some of the onlookers who gathered outside the McLean home to await his arrival. He seemed older and balder than wartime photographs showed him. But one eyewitness noted that he "never appeared more grandly heroic than on this occasion." He gave no hint of the sorrow or anger that undoubtedly filled his heart. "Those who watched his face to catch a glimpse of what was passing in his mind," another observer reported, could detect "no trace of his inner sentiments."

**The two commanders were polite and respectful to each other throughout the meeting and came to acceptable terms without argument.**

## Two Great Leaders

Grant's appearance was in marked contrast to his opponent's. His own dress uniforms had failed to arrive at his headquarters, so he had no choice but to wear a plain and dusty field uniform. The two great figures of the war greeted each other solemnly, taking seats near the fireplace as Grant reminded Lee that they had met before

## The War Winds Down

**T**he meeting at Appomattox Court House, Virginia, between Robert E. Lee and Ulysses S. Grant was the first of a series of formal surrenders by the Confederate States of America. In the months that followed, Confederate generals across the South laid down their arms, ending four long years of rebellion.

**April 26:** General Joseph Johnston (right) surrendered to General William Tecumseh Sherman (left) near Durham, North Carolina.

**May 4:** General Richard Taylor (son of Zachary Taylor, 12th president of the United States), surrendered at Citronelle, Alabama.

**May 26:** General Edmund Kirby Smith surrendered the Confederate Department of the Trans-Mississippi to General Edward R. S. Canby.

**June 23:** General Stand Watie (the Civil War's only Native American general) surrendered Cherokee forces in Oklahoma. Watie was the last Confederate general to surrender.

— during the U.S.–Mexican War, when both men were ambitious young officers.

Finally, they got down to business. As they agreed to peace terms, Grant's aide, Lieutenant Colonel Ely S. Parker, wrote them down. Lee inquired about his soldiers' horses and pistols, and Grant generously agreed to permit the men to keep them. Lee thanked Grant, saying that it would mean a great deal to them as they returned home to work their farms. Then both men sat in silence, the scratch of pen on paper the only sound in the room. Grant later recalled that Lee's expression had given no hint as to whether he was "glad that the end had finally come, or felt sad…and was too manly to show it." There was "no theatrical display," said one of the officers who crowded into the McLean parlor to witness the historic event. Another asked, "What man could have laid down his sword at the feet of a victorious general with greater dignity?"

When the papers were signed, Lee rose, shook

Grant's hand, and walked slowly to the front porch, looking to one eyewitness suddenly "older, grayer... very tired." Lee betrayed his emotions only then, clapping his hands together and calling loudly for an orderly when he could not find his horse, Traveller. He then rode slowly back to camp as his men surrounded him and offered their last tearful cheers and salutes. The war was finally over.

## Citizen Lee

Following the war, Lee and his family lived in Richmond, where they were visited by many former Confederate and Union soldiers. Lee urged them to return home to "help build up the shattered fortunes of our old state."

Lee, shown here in 1865, was indicted for treason following the war, but an outraged Grant threatened to resign if all charges against his former enemy were not dropped. Despite a loyalty oath signed in October 1865, Lee's U.S. citizenship was not restored until July 1975. Somehow his oath had remained hidden in Washington until 1970. (A government clerk found it while shuffling through some old papers.) Some scholars believe its disappearance was a blatant attempt to make Lee appear unrepentant.

Lee's estate, Arlington, across the Potomac River from Washington, D.C., became a national military cemetery in 1864.

# A National Cemetery

Union quartermaster general Montgomery Meigs was angry when Robert E. Lee quit the U.S. Army and later led a Confederate army in the Civil War. Their friendship before the war as lieutenants in the Army Corps of Engineers seemed to dissolve into thin air. Meigs's anger grew deeper as time passed and thousands of Union soldiers died in battles with Lee's army.

Meigs wanted revenge. He saw his chance in the war's fourth year, when he was told to find a new place to bury the dead from the latest campaign against Lee. He picked the Lee family home, a Virginia plantation near Washington, D.C., called Arlington.

Meigs knew his choice meant Lee could never live there again.

But he could not have known where his decision would lead. In the years to come, Lee's home would become the nation's greatest monument to its war dead: Arlington National Cemetery.

## Lee's Beloved Home

Lee loved Arlington. As a young soldier, whenever Lee returned to Arlington for vacations from far-off posts, he liked to lie in bed and read to his children. He would order them to tickle his feet. "No tickling, no story," he would say.

When his father-in-law died in 1857, Lee came home again. Arlington had fallen into a sad state of disrepair. The roof leaked; fences were down; the lawns were overgrown with bushes and weeds.

Lee's slaves at Arlington brought new life to the fields by planting corn and other grains under his direction. Lee worked hard, too, along with the Irish laborers he hired, fixing the roof and repairing fences. He managed money with care, renting land he could not use to others. And he began bringing Arlington back.

Arlington sat on the Virginia border. It was a beautiful spot atop a hill just across the Potomac River from the nation's capital. Standing at the front entrance, Lee could see the Capitol building in the distance.

A bitter foe of the Confederacy, Union quartermaster general Montgomery C. Meigs was responsible for providing everything the Federal troops needed to wage war, from backpacks to battleships.

## Leaving Arlington

When the Civil War started, Lee chose to support the Confederacy. Sadly, he knew he could not stay at Arlington.

Lee left his home on April 22, 1861. The next month, Union troops moved in, making Arlington the headquarters for the defense of Washington. Many of the Lees' possessions disappeared, including much of their George Washington collection. Several forts were built on the property.

In 1863, as the war raged on, freed slaves streamed into

Washington. The government built a town at Arlington to house thousands of them. It was called Freedmen's Village, and it included schools, homes, churches, and a hospital.

## Soldier's Cemetery

The first Union soldier was buried on the property on May 13, 1864. By the end of the year, more than 7,000 soldiers had been buried near him, an average of more than 30 a day.

When the war ended in 1865, Lee wanted to contribute to peace. He did not try to reclaim Arlington, knowing that doing so would make Northerners angry. He saw Arlington only two more times, from a distance, on visits to Washington.

Freedmen's Village closed after 30 years, leaving Arlington to be

what it remains today: a cemetery. As the years passed, more soldiers served in more wars, and many of them were buried there. With time, the neat rows of simple markers began to seem very special. Arlington now honors the thousands of men and women who have served the nation they helped create. Each year, about four million people come to visit.

Among the 260,000 people buried at Arlington is Montgomery Meigs, the quartermaster general responsible for making it a burial ground. His body lies not far from Mary Lee's old rose garden.

Lee is not buried at Arlington, but the house there has been restored as a memorial to him. For that reason — and even more for what Arlington represents — it seems certain that Lee would still feel very much at home.

The first soldiers were buried at Arlington National Cemetery in 1864. Since then, more than 260,000 people have been memorialized there, including two presidents.

# A School for Gentlemen

**O**n a chilly morning in early October 1865, Robert E. Lee began a new job and a new life in a new home. On that morning, the former Confederate general took the oath of office as president of Washington College, a small school in Lexington, Virginia. For the brief ceremony, Lee wore one of his gray army uniforms with the insignia removed; he had no other clothes.

## Raised From the Ashes

Washington College was in poor financial condition. It had only a handful of students and a faculty of but five professors. Its buildings and equipment were in bad shape. The year before, Union soldiers under General David Hunger had looted its library and damaged its buildings.

School opened that autumn with 50 students, but thanks to Lee's reputation, the number increased until the enrollment reached 400. Many who applied did not even know the name of the school and sent letters to "Lexington College," "Washington Institute," "Virginia University," or "General Lee's College."

## Educating a New Generation

Lee worked hard at his new job. As he wrote to his son Rooney, he wanted to "be of service to the country and the rising generation." Lee believed that the students should learn practical skills to help rebuild the South. Under his administration, the school started new fields of study, including departments of mechanical and civil engineering, practical mechanics, practical chemistry, and modern languages.

These new programs would require more professors, classrooms, and equipment. Although he disliked asking for money, Lee wrote a letter to Cyrus H. McCormick, the inventor of the reaper. McCormick, a native of Lexington, had moved to Chicago and become very wealthy. He responded with a check for $10,000 for a new classroom building and later sent additional contributions. Other Northern businessmen, impressed by Lee's ideas, donated money and books to the school.

Washington Hall, built in 1821, sits at the center of the campus. Washington and Lee University was originally founded in 1749 as Augusta Academy and is among the oldest colleges in the country.

## Students from the North and South

In the impoverished South, parents had to make great sacrifices to send their children to college. One boy, Harvey Butler Fergusson, walked all the way from Alabama carrying a gold watch and $300, all that his family could scrape together for his four years of college. The boy spent the summers in the Lexington area working as a field hand to help pay his expenses.

Lee knew each student at Washington College by name. Many were veterans who had served with him during the war. Such men often had a steadying influence on the younger boys. Lee received weekly reports on each student's classwork. If a boy had a problem, he was called into the president's office, where Lee gave him helpful advice. Though usually kind and gentle, Lee did not hesitate to expel any student who behaved badly and brought disgrace to the school. Lee did not believe in too many rules. Once, when asked by a couple of students for a copy of the school regulations, Lee told them, "We have no written rules. Each student

Sculptor Edward Valentine carved a memorial (right) depicting Lee resting before battle. The sculpture, completed in 1874, stands in the Lee Chapel (below).

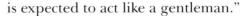

is expected to act like a gentleman."

Students from many Northern states also came to Washington College. As enrollment increased, the college chapel became too small to hold all the students. So Lee suggested that a new chapel be built. It was approved in July 1866. Lee's son Custis, who headed the engineering department at the nearby Virginia Military Institute, selected the design of the chapel, and Lee chose the site and supervised the construction. When it was finished, he moved his office to the basement of the chapel.

The years of war had put a strain on Lee's heart, and his responsibilities as college president took a further toll. His health gradually declined, and on October 12, 1870, he died of a stroke. He was entombed in a vault in the basement of the college chapel, a few feet from the room that had been his office. In his honor, the name of the school was changed to Washington and Lee University. To many people, however, it would always be "General Lee's College."

## "Only a Poor Old Confederate"

**O**n March 24, 1870, Lee and his daughter Agnes began what was supposed to be a quiet, relaxing sightseeing trip through the South by train. Four days into the trip, however, they were recognized and greeted by a Confederate veteran. From then on, cheering crowds and blaring bands greeted them at each station stop. Said the puzzled retired general, "Why should they care to see me? I am only a poor old Confederate." When the trip ended, he was physically exhausted from all the attention.

# CIVIL WAR

## 1860

### NOV 6
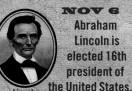
Abraham Lincoln is elected 16th president of the United States.

Lincoln

## 1861

### FEB 9

Formation of the Confederate States of America (CSA) by secessionist states South Carolina, Mississippi, Florida, Alabama, Georgia, Louisiana, and Texas. Jefferson Davis elected CSA president.

Davis

### MAR 4
Lincoln's inauguration

### APR 12

Fort Sumter  (South Carolina) Civil War begins with Confederate attack under Gen. Pierre Beauregard.

### APR 15
Lincoln issues proclamation calling for 75,000 troops. Gen. Winfield Scott becomes commander of Union army.

### APR 17
Virginia joins CSA, followed by Arkansas, Tennessee, and North Carolina.

### APR 20
Gen. Robert E. Lee resigns from U.S. Army and accepts command in Confederate army.

### JUL 21
First Manassas (Virginia) Gen. Thomas J. "Stonewall" Jackson defeats Gen. Irvin McDowell.

### NOV 1
Gen. George B. McClellan assumes command of Union forces.

## 1862

### FEB 11-16
Fort Donelson (Tennessee) Gen. Ulysses S. Grant breaks major Confederate stronghold.

### MAR
McClellan begins Peninsular Campaign, heading to Richmond, Virginia, the Confederate capital.

### APR 6-7
Shiloh (Tennessee) Grant defeats Beauregard and Gen. A.S. Johnston. Heavy losses on both sides.

### APR 24

New Orleans (Louisiana) Gen. David Farragut leads 17 Union gunboats up Mississippi River and takes New Orleans, the South's most important seaport.

### JUN 25-JUL 1
Seven Days (Virginia) Six major battles are fought over seven days near Richmond, Virginia. Lee is victorious, protecting the Confederate capital from Union occupation.

Halleck

### JUL 18
Lincoln turns over command to Gen. Henry W. Halleck.

### AUG 29-30
Second Manassas (Virginia) Jackson and Gen. James Longstreet defeat Gen. John Pope.

### SEP 17
Antietam (Maryland) McClellan narrowly defeats Lee. Bloodiest day in American military history: 23,000 casualties.

### SEP 22

Lincoln issues preliminary Emancipation Proclamation, freeing slaves in Confederate states.

### OCT 3-4
Corinth (Mississippi) Gen. William Rosecrans defeats Gen. Earl Van Dorn.

44

NOTE: Battles are in black type, with flags indicating: Union victory 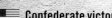 Confederate victory

# TIME LINE

**NOV 7**
Lincoln replaces McClellan with Gen. Ambrose Burnside to lead Army of the Potomac.

Burnside

**DEC 13**
Fredericksburg  (Virginia) Lee defeats Burnside.

## 1863

**JAN 1**
Final Emancipation Proclamation frees slaves in Confederate states. Union army begins enlisting black soldiers.

**JAN 25**
Lincoln replaces Burnside with Gen. Joseph Hooker.

Hooker

**JAN 29**
Grant is placed in command of the Union army in the West.

**MAY 1-4**
Chancellorsville (Virginia) Lee defeats Hooker.

**JUN 28**
Lincoln replaces Hooker with Gen. George E. Meade.

**JUL 1-3**

Gettysburg (Pennsylvania) Meade defeats Lee.

**JUL 4**
Vicksburg (Mississippi) After weeks of seige, Grant takes the Confederate stronghold on Mississippi River, effectively dividing eastern and western Confederate forces.

**SEP 18-20**
Chickamauga (Georgia) Gen. Braxton Bragg defeats Rosecrans.

**OCT 16**
Lincoln puts Grant in charge of all western operations.

**NOV 19**
Lincoln delivers the Gettysburg Address, dedicating the battlefield as a national cemetery.

**NOV 23-25**
Chattanooga (Tennessee) Grant defeats Bragg.

## 1864

**MAR 9**
Lincoln puts Grant in command of entire Union army. Gen. William T. Sherman takes over western operations.

**MAY 8-21**
Spotsylvania (Virginia) Grant defeats Lee.

**MAY 31-JUN 12**
Cold Harbor (Virginia) Lee defeats Grant and Meade.

**JUN 15-18**

Petersburg (Virginia) Lee and Beauregard defeat Grant and Meade.

**NOV 8**
Lincoln is re-elected.

**NOV 15-DEC 21**

Sherman's "March to the Sea." Sherman destroys supplies and transportation systems from Atlanta to Savannah (Georgia), crippling the Confederacy.

## 1865

Lee

**APR 2**
Petersburg (Virginia) Grant defeats Lee. Confederates leave Richmond.

**APR 9**
Lee surrenders to Grant at Appomattox Court House, Virginia.

**APR 14**
Lincoln is shot by John Wilkes Booth at Ford's Theatre, Washington, D.C. He dies the following morning.

**DEC 6**
Thirteenth Amendment to the Constitution abolishing slavery is ratified.

GRAPHICS BY FRED CARLSON

# Glossary

**Abolish:** To get rid of completely. An *abolitionist* works to end slavery.

**Affinity:** A natural attraction to, or feeling of connection with, someone or something.

**Amputation:** The removal, by surgery, of a body part such as an arm or leg.

**Arsenal:** A supply of weapons; also, a building in which weapons are stored.

**Artillery:** Heavy weapons, such as cannon. An *artilleryman* is a soldier who specializes in the use of artillery.

**Battery:** In the army, an artillery unit.

**Bondage:** Bound to serve another with practically no hope of freedom.

**Cadet:** A student at a military school who is training to be an officer.

**Campaign:** In military terms, a series of battles, or other operations, in a particular area to accomplish a specific goal.

**Cavalry:** A division of the army that fights on horseback.

**Commission:** In the military, the official authority as an officer, or a military assignment given to an officer.

**Confederacy:** In the American Civil War, the alliance of states that broke ties with the U.S. government to form a new government,

called the Confederate States of America. The states that did not secede supported the Union.

**Corps:** In the military, a separate combat division with a special assignment.

**Disdain:** A feeling or show of scorn or rejection.

**Emancipation:** Freedom from slavery or other form of bondage.

**Entourage:** A group of attendants who accompany a high-ranking person.

**Exemplary:** Worthy of imitation.

**Indict:** To formally accuse someone of wrongdoing, such as a crime.

**Infantry:** The branch of the military consisting of soldiers who are trained to fight on foot.

**Insignia:** A badge, or badges, of office, military rank, membership, or nationality.

**Insurrection:** An open revolt against the government or civil authority.

**Light horse:** A saddle horse; a horse bred primarily for riding, not pulling.

**Obscurity:** A state of being unknown or difficult to understand.

**Offensive:** In war, an attack or assault.

**Plantation:** A large estate, often

with resident workers, that produces income crops.

**Pneumonia:** A disease of the lungs that makes breathing very difficult.

**Quartermaster:** An officer responsible for the food, clothing, and equipment of troops.

**Secede:** To make a formal withdrawal from an organization, alliance, or, in American history, a nation. *Secession* occurred when 11 states officially withdrew from the United States of America and formed a new nation, the Confederate States of America.

**Skirmish:** A small conflict between enemies that can often lead to a larger battle.

**Spartan:** Simple, frugal, austere; the term refers to the people of Sparta, who were known for their courage, discipline, and restraint.

**Treason:** A deliberate action that betrays one's country, such as aiding its enemies.

**Tuberculosis:** A disease of the lungs that causes the sufferer to cough up mucus. Other symptoms include a high fever, chest pain, and weight loss.

**Union:** In the American Civil War, the states that supported the United States government. The states that did not support the U.S. seceded to form the Confederate States of America.

**Vanquish:** To defeat in a battle or competition; to conquer.

# Index

# COBBLESTONE®
# The CIVIL WAR Series

Few events in our nation's history have been as dramatic as those leading up to and during the Civil War. People held strong views on each side of the Mason-Dixon line, and the clash of North and South had far-reaching consequences for our country that are still being felt today.

Each 48-page book delivers the solidly researched content *COBBLESTONE®* is known for, written in an engaging manner that is sure to retain the attention of young readers. Perfect for report research or pursuing an emerging interest in the Civil War, these resources will complete your collection of materials on this important topic.

*Each sturdy, hardcover volume includes:*

- Fair and balanced depictions of people and events
- Well-researched text ■ Historical photographs
- Glossary ■ Time line

**$17⁹⁵ each**

| | |
|---|---|
| **NATION AT WAR:** SOLDIERS, SAINTS, AND SPIES | COB67900 |
| **YOUNG HEROES** OF THE NORTH AND SOUTH | COB67901 |
| **ABRAHAM LINCOLN:** DEFENDER OF THE UNION | COB67902 |
| **GETTYSBURG:** BOLD BATTLE IN THE NORTH | COB67903 |
| **ANTIETAM:** DAY OF COURAGE AND SACRIFICE | COB67904 |
| **ROBERT E. LEE:** DUTY AND HONOR | COB67905 |
| **ULYSSES S. GRANT:** CONFIDENT LEADER AND HERO | COB67906 |
| **STONEWALL JACKSON:** SPIRIT OF THE SOUTH | COB67907 |
| **JEFFERSON DAVIS** AND THE CONFEDERACY | COB67908 |
| **REBUILDING A NATION:** PICKING UP THE PIECES | COB67909 |

**Buy 3 books and get our Time Line Poster FREE!**

Our books are available through all major wholesalers, as well as directly from us.